The Portuguese Expedition to Abyssinia in 1541–1543

Miguel de Castanhoso

Of how D. Christovão pitched his Camp on the skirts of the Hill, and of how he took Order to attack it.

On the morning of the next day, February 1st, 1542, the eve of the day of the Purification of Our Lady, we pitched our camp, and as D. Christovão came with full knowledge of the approaches, as soon as we were in sight he allotted them to the Captains: to Francisco Velho and Manuel da Cunha, with their people and three pieces of artillery, the first approach, with the wall at the foot, the attack to be made at a given signal; to the second he appointed João da Fonseca and Francisco de Abreu, with three other pieces of artillery, and with the same instructions as to the signal; as the last approach was the strongest and most dangerous, he selected it for himself with the remaining people. There remained on guard over the Queen sixty soldiers with matchlocks and pikes, who were angry and discontented that they were excluded from the attack. That day also, late, D. Christovão made a feint of attacking, signalling to the Captains and bringing his artillery close, drawn up in order (*posse em ordem*); he did this to learn where it would be better to attack with matchlocks, and where the artillery would cause greater damage; and also to induce them to expend their munitions and magazines, which would help us on the following day. It is [34] difficult to believe how thick the stones and arrows fell when we got near; and they let fall rocks from the hill above, which caused us great fear and damage. When D. Christovão had seen all he wanted he retired. When the Moors saw this, it appeared to them that we could not attack them, and their delight was so excessive that all night they made great clamour with many trumpets and kettledrums. The Queen, too, became very sad and distrustful, for it seemed to her as it appeared to the Moors, that there was no more determination in us than that, for she had watched all. As D. Christovão, from what he was told, understood her distrust, he sent to tell her why he had advanced and retreated; and that in the morning her highness would see how the Portuguese fought, and what men they were. That night we spent in careful guard.

Of how the Portuguese attacked this Hill and captured it, with the Death of some.

At dawn, on the following day, we all commended ourselves to Our Lady, and made a general confession before a crucifix, held in his hands by a Mass priest, and received absolution from the patriarch; when this was done we fell into our ranks, and marched to the hill, each to his own pass, as had been before arranged. At D. Christovão's [35] signal we all attacked together, and our artillery helped us greatly, for it all fired high, and caused the Moors great fear, so that they dared not approach close to the edge of the hill, whence they could have wrought us much damage with a vast store of rocks; had it not been, as I say, for the artillery and matchlocks, which searched every place, they had killed many from the top, this helped us greatly. All the same, they treated us very badly, and killed two men of ours before we began to climb the hill. D. Christovão, seeing the evil treatment they gave us, attacked the ascent very briskly, and we all followed him with our lives in our hands; when we got under shelter of the hill the stone-throwing did us less harm, and then we began to ascend the pass. D. Christovão headed the climb by the help of his pike, and of fissures in the rocks; here many were wounded, and all twice beaten back, but our matchlocks kept off the Moors from approaching the pass. With this help we forced our way in, D. Christovão being among the first, and he certainly gave this day proof of his great courage, and it was his valour that rendered the capture of the pass easy. The Moors were so hard pressed that the commander had not time to mount his horse; when he saw the Portuguese on the summit, he prepared, with his five hundred companions, to defend themselves, animating and urging them to advance; but with all they could not await the impetuosity of the Portuguese. At the time these Moors gave way, Manuel da Cunha and Francisco Velho were already on the top with their following, the forcing costing them much labour. They suffered a good deal, and many Portuguese were wounded before they [36] entered the outer gate; between the two gates the Moors slew two Portuguese. The Moors would not close the last gate, thinking they could take better vengeance inside. When our men did get in, they found them formed up in one body, with the commander and three others on horseback. Our men, seeing them collected together, attacked with the shout of "St. James!" falling on with lance-thrusts and sword-cuts, and the battle raged. The commander at this pass fought like a very valiant man. He ran a Portuguese through with a javelin he carried, transfixing him through his armour; then he drew his sword, and delivered such a blow on another's head that he dashed his helmet into his skull and felled him to the ground senseless. Seeing then the destruction that Moor wrought, three attacked him at once, threw him down, and he died the death he deserved. While this was in progress, the third pass of Joao da Fonseca and Francisco de Abreu was entered, with the same opposition as the others; and in the forcing they slew two of their men. When the Moors saw the passes were occupied they retreated, the one body on the other, neither knowing of the other's defeat; thus they all collected under our swords and pikes, and remained in a trap whence none escaped. Those who had fled early hid in the houses, and were all killed by the Abyssinians, who delighted in doing it. Some Moors preferred to throw themselves from the summit, hoping they might escape; but they were all dashed to pieces. After the capture of the hill, we searched the houses, where we found many captive Christian women and many other Moor women. We also captured nine horses and ten

[37] very handsome mules, besides many others, perhaps seventy or eighty. When we mustered, we found a loss of eight Portuguese, who had been killed in the attack, and over forty wounded. D. Christovão went straight to the mosque after the victory, and directed the patriarch and the padres who had followed to consecrate it, in order that Mass might be said the next day. They gave it the name of Our Lady of Victory, and we buried there the eight Portuguese. D. Christovão next sent to ask the Queen if she wished to see the hill in the condition in which the Moors had held it. She was astonished at the ease with which we had carried it; she considered that all the Moors who were on the summit could not possibly be killed. When she was told by her people that it was true, she said that indeed we were men sent of God, and she thought all things were possible to us, but that she did not wish to ascend the hill, as the road was so full of dead bodies that it would pain her. When everything had been arranged, D. Christovão came to the Queen, leaving on the summit those wounded who could not be moved, as they were weary and their wounds cold. The Queen gave the hill to one of her Captains, whose ancestors had held it. The name of the hill is Baçanete. We spent the whole month here resting, in order to cure the wounded. As the news spread over the country, the inhabitants came to us with ample supplies, and with all that we needed. At the end of February, before we left here, there joined us two Portuguese with six Abyssinians to guide them, sent by Manuel de Vasconcellos, who was in Massowa in command of five ships, sent by D. Estevão from India, to learn what had happened to us; whether we needed any help or anything, as we should be provided with all. [38] D. Christovão, in particular, and we all were much pleased at this news; and Francisco Velho was at once ordered to get ready with forty men, to go to Manuel de Vasconcellos and give him letters for the Governor, his brother; and in the same bundle

were enclosed letters for the King, our lord, in which he reported to him the country he had reduced to obedience to the Queen, that is, about forty leagues, and this merely through dread of the Portuguese name. They also went to the fleet, to bring back the powder and the munitions necessary for the war. When Francisco Velho had started, the Queen and D. Christovão determined to shift their camp to eight leagues away: to some plain country where supplies were very abundant, as the lord there was a Christian, and had become subject to the Moors against his will. He wrote to the Queen to invite her, as she would be better supplied there, for he was and always had been hers. He explained his obedience to the Moor as extracted from him by force, and asked her pardon. We marched there to await the Portuguese, who should not take more than fifteen days in [39] coming and going, as they travelled on very free-going mules, and only carried their arms, and there was no reason for longer delay.

Of how D. Christovão in nearing the plains of Jarte, met an Ambassador from the Preste, and of the Warning received that the King of Zeila was near.

We had marched for two days towards Jarte (*para o jarte*) which is the lordship of that Captain I mentioned, when, while we were pitching our camp, there arrived an envoy from the Preste, with a message for the Commander to march as quickly as might be, while he did the same, in order to join before meeting the King of Zeila, who had a large force, and with whom a fight by one alone would be perilous. Thus we marched on until we reached the plains, where came the Captain of the country, to ask pardon and pity of the Queen, who pardoned him, for she had had many communications from him, and knew that he was always a Christian. He visited D. Christovão, and presented him with four very handsome horses, and told him that he knew that the King of Zeila was coming in search of us, and that many days could not elapse before we met him; that he should make what arrangements were necessary, and that he himself would send out spies to discover what was occurring. D. Christovão asked him to do this, and determined to march slowly, [40] awaiting our men, fearing lest the King of Zeila should come on us before we joined the Preste. We marched forward in this way, with many spies ahead of us, who two days later returned to us with the news that the Moors' camp was near, and that we should meet before the next day. When D. Christovão found that he could not avoid a battle with the Moors without losing the reputation we had gained, he determined to accept it; for he felt, concerning the country people, that if he retreated to the hill they would disobey him, and would not assist him with any supplies; and that it was far the greater risk to chance famine, and losing our prestige, than to fight the Moors, for victory is in the hands of God. With minds made up we continued our march, and when we reached some wide plains two horsemen, who had been ahead scouting the plain, returned, saying that the King of Zeila was a league away. We at once pitched our camp, and it was the Saturday before Palm Sunday. D. Christovão, as the Queen came in the rear, and had heard how near the enemies were, went out to receive her with great parade and joy, for she was a woman, and came filled with fear at the news. Encouraging her greatly, he placed her in the centre of our camp, which was this same day pitched in proper order, and arranged to await in it the Moors; for the ground was very suitable, as we occupied the best site on the plain, for we were on a hillock in it. All the night [41] we watched vigilantly, and the following morning, at dawn, there appeared on the summit of a hill five Moorish horsemen, who were spying the plain; when they saw us they retired to give the news to the King. Then D. Christovão sent two Portuguese on good horses to ascend the hill, and discover how large the enemy's camp was, and where pitched; they returned directly, saying that they covered the plains and were halted close to the hill. While his camp was being pitched, the King of Zeila ascended a hill with several horse and some foot to examine us; he halted on the top with three hundred horse and three large banners, two white with red moons, and one red with a white moon, which always accompanied him, and by which he was recognised; thence he examined us, while the rest of his army, with its bannerets, descended the hill and surrounded us. Such was their trumpeting, drumming, cries, and skirmishing, that they appeared more numerous and stout-hearted [than they were]. D. Christovão, thinking they meant to attack us, visited all the defences. We were ready for the fight; but they did no more than hold us surrounded all that day and that night, lighting many fires everywhere, and with the same noise and music. We feared them greatly that night, for every moment we thought they would attack us. We stood ready and armed, with powder-pots in our hands, matches lighted for the artillery and matchlocks, firing from time to time the bases as a guard, for we feared much their horse-men. We learned afterwards, from the Abyssinians who were with them, that they dared not attack us at night because our camp appeared from the outside very formidable, both because of the shots we fired from time to time, and [42] because of the many matches they saw lighted, of which they had great fear; they said it could not be we were so few as we appeared by day.

Of the Embassy the King of Zeila sent to D. Christovão.

After this night, passed in trouble, as I tell, on the morning of the next day, the King of Zeila sent a king-at-arms to D. Christovão with a message: that he marvelled greatly how he had the audacity to appear before him with so small a force; that indeed he seemed to be a mere boy, as rumour said, and innocent without experience. As he had been so deceived, he did not blame him, but the people of the country, who knew the truth. That they, indeed, were of small account, for they were disloyal to their own King. That he knew in fact that that woman had beguiled him, but that he should pay no more attention to her. That he, as a pitiful King, wished to have compassion on him, and for his boldness in facing him (a thing which had not happened in fourteen years in that country), he would pardon his great temerity, on condition that he came over to him with all his Portuguese. That if he did not care to join him, that he could return to his own country. That he assured him no evil should befall him. That he treated him with this magnanimity because of his age and inexperience, and because he was sure that the woman had deluded him, by telling him that in those countries there was some other King than himself; but, since he now knew the truth, that he should do as he [43] was ordered. With this he sent him a friar's cowl and a rosary of beads, making us all out friars — for so they call us. After D. Christovão had heard the King's message, he gave great honour and welcome to him who brought it, and gave him a red' satin garment, and a scarlet cap with a valuable medal; and told him to return and he would send a reply to the King. Dismissing him, he had him accompanied out of the camp, and then discussed with the Captains and fidalgos what reply he should send to the Moor, and who should take the answer. It was agreed not to send a Portuguese — as there was no trusting a Moor — but a boy of a Portuguese, his slave and white. He was clothed finely, and given a mule to ride. His answer was a few lines written in Arabic, that the King might read it. This said that he had come here by order of the great Lion of the Sea, who is very powerful on land; whose custom it is to help those who are helpless and need his assistance. That as he was informed that the most Christian King, the Preste, his brother in arms, had been defeated and driven from his kingdom by the infidels and enemies of our Holy Catholic Faith, he had sent the small succour that was here, which still sufficed against such evil and bad persons; that reason and justice, which were on his side, were enough to defeat them, as they only conquered that country because our Lord desired to chastise the Abyssinians for their sins. That he trusted that in future they would be free, and would recover possession of what they had had. That the following day he would see what the Portuguese were worth, and that was not to go over to him; for they obeyed no lord save the King of Portugal, [44] whose vassals all the Kings of India, Arabia, Persia, and the greater part of Africa were; and the same, by the help of our Lord, he hoped to make him. With this he sent him small tweezers for the eyebrows, and a very large looking-glass — making him out a woman. The slave carried this message, but it did not please the Moor; still, he said that people of such stomach, who though few yet wanted to fight him, were worthy that all Kings should do them much honour and favour. With this the slave returned. The Moor determined to continue the blockade, to see if he could not reduce us by famine. That day he did no more than hold us besieged, and creep somewhat closer to us. There were fifteen thousand foot, all archers and bucklermen; fifteen hundred horse, and two hundred Turkish arquebusiers, of whom they thought a great deal, and with whom they had conquered all that country. They were indeed men of greater determination, for they came closer to us than any of the others, and helped him a good deal. They got so close that they made some breastworks of loose stones very near us, whence they did us some hurt. D. Christovão had to send Manuel da Cunha and Inofre de Abreu with seventy men to dislodge them, which they did. The horsemen tried to support the Turks, and here some Portuguese were wounded. From the camp our artillery killed some horsemen, and wounded many Moors. D. Christovão, finding that this engagement increased, ordered a trumpet to sound the recall, and they obeyed; thus the day passed. That night D. Christovão determined (as our supplies were failing, and the Captain of the country who was with us was unable to help us, as we were blockaded) to join battle next morning early, as they refused to attack. Thus we passed the night with careful watch, and before dawn we began to get ready. [45]

Of how D. Christovão fought the first Battle with the King of Zeila, in which the Moor was defeated and wounded by a matchlock Bullet.

After the artillery had been mounted on the carriages, and the tents and all the baggage loaded on mules, D. Christovão arranged his forces: the Captains with their men were in advance, the Queen with her women and all the transport in the centre, and the royal standard, with the rest of the force, in the rear; thus we made a circle as we were surrounded on all sides; the arrangements were completed before dawn without our being discovered. At break of day, on Tuesday, April 4, 1542, we began to march towards the enemy. D. Christovão, with eight mounted Portuguese and four or five Abyssinians, visited every part of the force, arranging the men. When the Moors saw us advancing towards them, they raised such a noise of shouting, trumpets, and kettle-drums, that it seemed as if the world were dissolving; they showed great joy, thinking they had us already in their net. At this we began to do our duty with matchlocks and artillery, which played continually on all sides, so that we cleared the plain as we advanced. [46] The Turks, who were in our front, seeing the damage we caused, advanced close to us, and the battle began to rage. When the Moor found that the Turks were those who helped him most, he came in person against us with more than five hundred horse, and with the three standards that were always with him. Here we found ourselves in great trouble; but our artillery stood us in good stead, for those in charge behaved like valiant men without fear, and fired so rapidly that the horse could never get near us, because the horses feared the fire; still the Moors did us much harm, especially the

Turks with their matchlocks. D. Christovão, seeing this, halted the force, ordering us not to fight save with the artillery, with which we did them much hurt; and as one hundred Turks advanced very close to us, D. Christovão sent Manuel da Cunha to attack them with his men, that is, about fifty Portuguese. He obeyed, and the engagement waxed so fierce that the Turks seized the banner and slew the ensign and three other Portuguese; they also killed and wounded many of the Turks; Manuel da Cunha retired, wounded in the leg with a matchlock bullet. All this while D. Christovão was encouraging our people, always present where danger was greatest, many of ours being wounded; he himself was wounded by another bullet in the other leg, which was a great disaster for all, but for him an honour, for, wounded as he was, he behaved himself and acted as we find no example of any notable Captain in ancient or modern histories. The battle going thus, as I say, and it being now midday, it pleased the Lord God to remember His servants, as He always does in times of such dire distress, when He is merciful. It [47] appeared to us that we had the worst of the battle, and it appeared to the King of Zeila, who saw it from the outside, the opposite. He therefore advanced to encourage his men, and came so close to us that he was wounded in the thigh by a matchlock bullet, that pierced his horse, which fell dead under him. When they saw him fall, his ensigns lowered the three banners which accompanied him: this was the signal of retreat; they lowered them three times, and then took him up in their arms and bore him away. When D. Christovão saw this he knew that the Moor had been wounded; then sounding the trumpets and kettle-drums, we shouted "St. James!" and charged, with the Abyssinians who were with us, in number about two hundred. We slew many and followed them a space, where the Abyssinians avenged themselves on the Moors, slaying them as if they had been sheep. D. Christovão, as he had no horse to pursue, and as we were all very weary, and as we feared lest the Moorish horse should turn on us, contented himself with the victory our Lord had given him that day, which was not a small one. While we were in pursuit, the Queen had had a tent pitched and placed the wounded in it; she and her women went about binding up the wounded with their own head-gear, and weeping with pleasure at the great mercy our Lord God had done them that day, for truly she had found herself in great fear and tribulation. Meanwhile, D. Christovão returned to where the tent was pitched, and had all the others pitched also. The dead on the battle-field were examined, to bury the Portuguese who had fallen. There were eleven, and among them Luiz Rodriguez de Carvalho, with a musket-ball through the head, the first man killed, Lopo da Cunha fidalgo, and a foster-brother of D. Christovão; there were [48] over fifty wounded, chiefly by matchlock bullets; but the enemy paid heavily, for the field was full of them; among them the Abyssinians recognised four of the principal Captains of the King of Zeila; there lay dead on the field forty horses and thirty Turks. After we had buried the dead we wanted to rest; but the Captain of that country said to D. Christovão that we should not stay on that spot, as water was scarce, and there was little grass for the mules; that we should approach the skirts of a range of hills two matchlock shots away, where water was plentiful, and where we should be lords of the country, through which abundant supplies could come from his territory, and the enemy unable to interfere. This was agreed to, and, after eating, we left that spot and went there. This day D. Christovão laboured much, for he attended to all the wounded himself; for the surgeon we had with us was wounded in the right hand. After attending to all the others, he tended his own wound last of all. When night fell, he sent a man very secretly, to travel night and day until he came up with the Portuguese who were in Massowa, to tell them of the victory and of the King's wound, and to direct them to hasten, as he hoped in God to be able, on their arrival, to finish the conquest. We stayed here, curing the wounded and resting, until the first Sunday after Easter, both because the wounded could not carry arms, and in order to see if the Portuguese came. After Easter and its octave had passed, D. Christovão, seeing that there was delay, and that the enemy would meanwhile be enabled to recruit their army, determined to fight a second battle on the Sunday, for we were in sight of each other. It was [49] in this battle that the patriarch and others first saw the blessed St. James help us, in the shape in which he always does; there can be no doubt but that without his help, and chiefly that of our Lord, we should never have been victorious.

Of the Second Battle which D. Christovão fought with the King of Zeila, in which the King was defeated.

Thus, when the Sunday after Easter came, the camp was struck before dawn, and all were drawn up in order, with the artillery in its place, and the Queen with her women in the centre. After the patriarch had said the general confession and absolved us, we marched against the Moors, who when they saw us also advanced. The King, still suffering from his wound, lay on a bed carried on men's shoulders. He came to encourage his men, but this was hardly necessary, for they were so numerous that merely seeing how few we were encouraged them; besides, there had joined him a Captain with five hundred horse and three thousand foot; and had we delayed longer many more would have come to him; for his Captains were scattered over the country, and, when he was wounded, he called them all in, and they joined him daily. The Captain [50] who had come in was called Grada Amar, and it was he who was the first to attack us. He, too, urged on the others, saying, how could so few as we were endure long against such a force. In his pride he attacked us with five hundred horse, and had all his men followed his example they would indeed have done us much hurt; but from dread of the artillery, which slew many, they could not break our ranks; but the Captain with four or five valiant Moors threw themselves on our pikes and died like brave cavaliers. D. Christovão all this time kept everything in the best possible order, and everyone fought with great courage; but had the horse broken our ranks then our destruction was a certainty: for when this Captain attacked with his horse, all the others who were on horseback did the like from all sides. By the will of our Lord, at this time, a little powder accidentally caught fire in the part where we were weakest. Truly we thought we should all be burned when we saw the fire in the powder, but as it told for our victory, we did not notice the loss it caused: that is, two Portuguese killed and eight burned, who were very badly injured. The horsemen could not [51] break in because of the fire I mention, as the horses were so frightened that they bolted over the plain with their riders. Meanwhile, we did our duty both with the artillery and the matchlocks, and the whole field was strewn with corpses. Eight Portuguese who were mounted did such deeds, that had they been done at any other time, they would have been held in remembrance. I will not name them, because the footmen would have done the same had they had horses; their deeds while on foot prove this, for they went out to the Turks who came near us, and fought grandly: so that they drove them back far, leaving many dead and wounded on the field. When the Turks retired, and the horse ho longer came on, D. Christovão saw that they were shaken; and we attacked them briskly, and drove them before us till they took flight. The victory would have been complete this day had we had only one hundred horses to finish it: for the King was carried on men's shoulders on a bed, accompanied by horsemen, and they fled with no order. D. Christovão pursued them for half a league, and killed many Moors, who in their haste took no thought of their camp and tents, which spoil fell to our lot. When we could no longer pursue the Moors, as we were very weary, we returned, and when we were mustered fourteen Portuguese were found missing, who were sought out and buried. As the grass on this plain was destroyed, D. Christovão and the Queen agreed to advance to camp by a stream that was near, to rest there, where there was more refreshment for the wounded, of whom there were more than sixty, and of these four or five subsequently died. We began our march, leaving the plain strewn with dead. [52] There was killed in this fight an Abyssinian Captain who was with us: a very valiant man. When we arrived in sight of the stream we saw the Moors halted on its banks, because, when they had crossed it the King thought that we were not in pursuit; and as it was late and the place suitable, he desired to rest there. They fled when they saw us; and an Abyssinian who joined us there, and who had been with them, told us afterwards that the King said "these *frades* will not let me long alone" — for thus they call us. The Moors started on their way, travelling all that night and eight days, without resting, and many who were wounded died on the march. As D. Christovão would not pursue he went no further, but we pitched our camp there, tending our wounded. Two days later, the Portuguese who had gone to Massowa returned, and with them the Barnaguais, with thirty horsemen and five hundred foot, whom we welcomed with much joy; but the Portuguese returned sadder than can be believed, because they were absent from the battles, and because they had not succeeded in the business on which they had gone, nor had even seen our fleet, because of the Turkish galleys who guarded the harbour, in order that our foists should learn nothing of us, nor we of them.

Of how, on the arrival of the Barnaguais and of the Portuguese, D. Christovão followed in pursuit of the King of Zeila.

D. Christovão was much rejoiced at the arrival of these men, and determined to pursue the Moor. He began his preparations at once, sending fourteen very badly wounded [53] Portuguese (of whom, as I have said, four or five died) to a hill governed by a Captain who was with us, called Triguemahon, who is like a Viceroy; he went with us to the hill, and we were all on beds, which was a heavy labour to those who carried us. Truly, the hospitality and honour we received from his wife and from himself cannot be expressed: for we were all so well provided and so well tended that in the houses of our own fathers we should have had no better, and I enlarge on this, for I was present. When, a month later, some of us were better, we returned to D. Christovão, for, directly he sent us to recover, he started in pursuit of the Moor. It took him ten days to reach where he was, which was in a great and strong hill, opposite the entrance to the straits, because he did not dare to retire elsewhere, for the country people after his defeat refused to obey him or give him supplies; and hence it suited him to retire to this hill, where he could recuperate, and could get assistance from the skirts of the sea, either from his own people or from the Turks, as it happened. Here, then, D. Christovão came up with him, and that with great labour, by reason of the rains and the mire, for the winter begins here at the end of April until September, as in India. And because, as I have said, the winter was beginning, it appeared better to the Queen to occupy another hill, which is called Ofala, in [54] sight of this one, and winter there, for now all the country people obeyed her, and in that country there were ample supplies; further, it was on the road by which the Preste would come, and it might be that he would arrive soon. This seemed good to D. Christovão, and he determined to send a man to the Preste to acquaint him with the victory in the battles, that with this encouragement he might march more quickly. And when he had written he sent a mulatto, called Ayres Dias, who knew the language of the country well, for he had been there in the time of D. Rodrigo de Lima, the Ambassador; he sent this man because by reason of his colour and of his tongue he might pass for a Moor. He reached the Preste, who was very pleased to hear what had occurred. The Queen collected many cultivators to make straw huts to winter in, which they made very diligently, for there are plenty of materials for this in the country, namely wood and straw; they also brought all the necessary supplies in great abundance, for the soil is very fertile and the produce great. The King of Zeila finding that, by reason of his defeat, those of the country refused to obey him or give supplies, had of necessity to send to take them by force; but his people returned each time fewer than they started, thus his only resource was what came to him from the skirts of the sea, which was very little. We could not intercept this, for the hill is very extensive, bounding all that country, so that he was the lord of the further side. He made up his mind, [55] finding the straits he was in, with his people dead or cowed, to send secretly to demand help from the Captain of Azebide, who was under the Turk, with three thousand Turks under him, sending to inform him of his defeat, and to tell him to regard him as a vassal of the Grand Turk, and not allow him to lose what he had already gained; with this he sent him much money, both for himself and for the Turks, of whom on this inducement there came nine hundred, all arquebusiers, very fine and good men; he also sent him ten field bombards, knowing that what damage he had received from us was by artillery and matchlocks, for hitherto he had had no field pieces. There also came to him many Arabs, sent by an Arabian lord, his friend; among these were twenty Turkish horsemen, with gilt stirrups, and their horses shod with iron, for in the Preste's country the horses go unshod. All this help came in the course of the winter without its being known.

Of what D. Christovão did that Winter, and of how he Captured a very strong Hill which had belonged to a Jew Captain.

About this time D. Christovão learnt that there was near us a hill of the Jews, by which the Preste must of necessity pass as there was no other road; that it had been captured by the Moors; and that the Captain of it, who was a Jew, was a fugitive because he obeyed the Preste; he put himself on the defensive when the Moors attacked the hill, and when he found they had captured it he fled. D. Christovão desired greatly to see him, to enquire what Moors were on the hill, and to discover if it could be recaptured. While in this mind the Jew, who had heard that he was wintering there with the Queen, determined to visit him to see if he could recover his country; because, from the information which he had of us, it seemed to him that this might be the case. Besides, our Lord chose to arrange matters thus, because the restoration of the kingdom was to be brought about by this means; when he came, the Jew informed D. Christovão about the hill, and told him that there were but few Moors on it, and that he would guide him to an approach where he would not be discovered until he was at the top, and that it was easy to capture, if the people of the country helped; that he would find on it many and good horses that were bred on the hill; and that it was quite impossible for the Preste in any manner to pass save over it, and that he had with him so [57] little strength that he could not capture it; when he had retired thence to the part whence he was now about to return, the hill had not yet been occupied by the Moors: had it been, he could not

have escaped. When D. Christovão learnt how small a force the Preste
had with him, he became very dispirited and disquieted, and went to the
Queen to learn if it was true that her son had so small a force; when it
was confirmed by her he became still more downcast, without, however,
letting her know it, because until then he had not heard this, but had
hoped that the Preste would quickly join him, as the winter was already
verging to an end. That he [the Preste] might not find that obstacle in
the way, and because he himself wanted the horses, he determined to go
there personally, as the Jew told him that with one hundred good followers he might with skill recover the hill; that he required but few days for
this, and that he could return to his camp with many horses without his
absence being noted. D. Christovão did not wish to take all his force to
capture that hill, lest the King of Zeila should think we were raising the
siege and leaving. If he did this, the Moors would advance and capture
the hill on which they [we] then were, and collect supplies of which they
had need; and it might be that they would pursue him, thinking he was
retreating; and, encouraged by this, they might have a confused and ill-
timed battle; it would allow them, too, to recover their boldness, which
had been much diminished by their late fear. That events might not so
fall out, he determined to carry out the expedition in another way to
leave the camp well guarded, and to go so secretly as not to be discovered, taking with him Manuel da Cunha and João da Fonseca and one
hundred men at the outside. He started at midnight, and travelled very
secretly, carrying with him many skins necessary for crossing a river near
the hill. They marched thus until they reached it, when they found it
much swollen. [58] They quickly cut a quantity of wood and branches,
and with these, and the skins filled with air, made rafts (*jangadas*), which
they bound strongly together, and for this they had brought the necessaries. They crossed a few at a time, taking their matchlocks, powder,

and matches inside other skins, lest they should be wetted; thus they all got over, some by swimming. When they and the mules had all crossed, they began to climb the hill, not being discovered until they were at the top. When the Moors saw them they armed quickly; there were about three thousand foot and four hundred horse. D. Christovão, who rode with the other eight Portuguese who were mounted, Manuel da Cunha on the one flank, with thirty matchlockmen, João da Fonseca on the other, with another thirty, and the remaining forty in the centre with the royal standard, attacked with great vigour. The Captain of the Moors, by name Cide Amede, advanced in front of his men and encountered D. Christovão, in which encounter he died; the other horsemen with D. Christovão also overcame each his man. By this time the foot had all collected into one body, and did nothing save slay the Moors; who, seeing their Captain dead, and that there was none before whom they could feel shame, nor from whom they could receive orders, took to flight, and many died, for the very Jews slew them, and few escaped. When the hill was cleared, D. Christovão collected the spoil, which was rich in goods [59] and slaves all very valuable. There were eighty excellent horses, with which he was more pleased than with anything else, and more than three hundred mules, with many cattle without number. When this was ended, he made over the hill to the Jew who had held it before, as he had always obeyed the Preste. When that Jew saw this great deed, and how God favoured us, he became a Christian, with twelve of his brethren, all Captains of places on that hill, which is twelve leagues long and all very fertile, with many populous places and villages and very strong; there are only two passes to it, all the rest is scarped rock. There are about ten thousand or twelve thousand Jews on it; it is four leagues across; on the summit are very pleasant valleys and streams, and by the skirts of the hill runs a river as large as the Douro, called Tagacem, the one crossed by D. Christovão; it runs all round the hill, which is almost made an island by it. It is the most fertile hill that can be, and they may boast that they still enjoy manna, since they are in such luxury that they can get honey from the rifts in the rocks, and there is so much that there is no owner, and whoever likes collects it. This hill lies nearly due west of the Straits, and may be forty leagues distant. When D. Christovão had made over the hill to the Jew, he left him an order to send to the Preste to inform him of its capture. He started for the camp, and as the way after passing the river was rough, he left thirty men with the horses to come on slowly, while he went on very quickly with the other seventy, dreading lest some disaster [60] should have befallen us, travelling both night and day. The very night he returned, the Turks arrived to reinforce the King of Zeila, and on the following day they mustered over one thousand matchlockmen. They came at once to the foot of our hill, and pitched their camp close to ours; thence they saluted us with their artillery and matchlocks, and pitched some balls into our camp. When D. Christovão saw this, he knew what succour had reached them, and took counsel with all as to what should be done. It was agreed to wait until the following day, when they could see the power of the Moor, but that they should not fight before the arrival of the horses, which could not be delayed more than two days: that, should the Moor attack us, we should defend ourselves the best we could, as our camp was somewhat fortified by some palisades erected during the winter. D. Christovão agreed to this, for he knew that, if we struck our camp that night, the very people would rise against us, and we should have nothing to eat; for this reason we were bound to fight and retain what we had gained. He sent an urgent message to those with the horses, to march as quickly as possible, as the Moors had been reinforced by the Turks, and a battle appeared imminent. We kept careful watch all that night, which was not good refreshment for those who came weary from their journey. All that night we were under arms.

Of how there was a Battle between D. Christovão and the King of Zeila, in which D. Christovão was defeated.

The next day, in the morning, Wednesday, August 28th, 1542, the day of the beheadal of St. John the Baptist, the [61] Moor came out with all his power, with one thousand Turks in advance, to give us battle: the artillery was in the van, all prepared. D. Christovão, seeing his intentions, manned the positions in the best way he could, and stood on the defensive. At daybreak the artillery began to play, for at that hour they advanced against us; by it and the matchlocks many on both sides were wounded. The Turks, as they were many and but recently arrived, advanced very proudly, doing us much hurt. When D. Christovão saw the great hurt they did us, and that the palisades of our camp were not strong enough to be defended, especially from the Turks, he decided to sally out frequently and attack them, and then retreat. It appeared to him that in this way he would secure victory, for they could not await the very first onset of any body of Portuguese. He acted accordingly: he being the very first who, with fifty soldiers, with matchlocks and pikes, attacked over one hundred Turks who were on that flank. He drove them back a considerable way, killing and wounding many. He began to retreat when he met the main body of the enemy, and in the retreat they killed four of his men; the remainder all returned wounded, including D. Christovão himself, with a matchlock bullet in one leg. When he had returned, Manuel da Cunha, as he had been ordered, attacked on the other side, and drove the Turks back for another space: for they were those who came closest to us and pressed us hardest. He, too, killed and wounded many, but in the retreat they killed five or six of his men, and wounded several. The other [62] captains of the positions, as one retreated another attacked, but always in the retreat they killed some of our men. The affair became so confused that they killed some of our men in the very camp. In this way we continued for a great part of the day; the followers of the Moor were pleased enough, seeing the Turks on their side, and the hurt we received. D. Christovão, wounded as he was, went round the positions, encouraging the men: for these are the days when leaders are recognised; I have no words wherewith even to express his courage, when looking at the positions and the camp, he saw his men very weary, and the greater number wounded. The Queen was in her house in the direst trouble, weeping for the hour that had come to her. The house was filled with men too wounded to fight, and she, with her women — who that day did their duty in this well — bound up their wounds. They fired many shot into her house, and wounded two of her women. When D. Christovão saw this, and the great hurt the Turks were causing, and that in each retreat men were killed, he ordered Francisco de Abreu to attack with his men on his side, and his brother, Inofre de Abreu, to follow on his flank, so that when the first retreated the other should support, that they might not have the opportunity of doing so much hurt. He attacked, killing many of them, but in the retreat his fortune willed that they killed him by a matchlock bullet. When his brother saw this, he ran to bring him in, forcibly driving them off; lifting his brother to carry him, a shot struck him and stretched him on the other; thus they both lay. Our men retreated with difficulty, for here they met the main body of the [63] Moors, who slew many of them. D. Christovão, seeing that they had slain the greater part of his people, collected whom he could — and they but few — round the royal standard: for there were not many now to fight, for midday was past. When they were collected, he left word with Manuel da Cunha to attack the Moors with his men during his retreat, to hinder their harming him; and he charged them straight, driving them back over the field a great space. Truly, had we had the horses, which were on the way, the victory was ours; but we deserved for our sins that this should befall us, to happen what did happen. While our men attacked they drove them like sheep, but they were now so weary they could not bear the fatigue. When D. Christovão turned to retreat he was so far in the field, that in the retreat they killed many of his men and wounded him with another bullet that broke his right arm; and he returned in great pain. Here Manuel da Cunha helped greatly, for he attacked the Moors, and then retreated with him; they also slew and wounded many of his. João da Fonseca, who had sallied from his position to drive off the Moors, was, after two or three sallies, killed, and Francisco Velho the same. When D. Christovão found that they had killed four of his Captains, and that the rest of his people, as well as himself, were so badly wounded, he determined to sally out no more, but continued encouraging his men, and trying to induce them to return to the positions, which now had none to guard them, and none to fight in them, for it grew very late. At this time the Turks entered the positions, and twice they were driven out; but, as matters stood, there was none to rally to the royal standard. When the patriarch saw affairs in this state, he mounted a mule, and retreated to a hill on our flank. The Queen wanted to do [64] the same, but D. Christovão ordered her to be restrained, lest the Portuguese should accompany her. By now many of the Moors were inside the palisades, and of ours there was none to fight, the greater part being wounded or dead. We were compelled to retreat up the hill, which D. Christovão refused, being determined to die. Our men, seeing that it served no purpose to delay, as there was none to fight, made him retreat, telling him that he could see that all the Portuguese were withdrawing, and that those around him were too few to resist the enemy; that, for all this, they would all die with him, as honour bade them, but that it would be wiser to join his own men, as the Lord God was pleased to give them that punishment for the sin of all. With this they made him retreat, riding a mule; the Queen preceding him, ready to share whatever fate befell us. With great labour we retreated up the hill, for we were all wounded, each one going as he could. The steepness of the hill was our safeguard, as horsemen could only follow us slowly; but the foot did us much hurt, as numbers followed us, and slew many who could not travel with arrows and stones. When night fell, some went one way, some another, without waiting the one for the other. D. Christovão went one way with the fourteen Portuguese, who always accompanied him, and the Queen another, with the rest of us; we continued our retreat in this confusion, and in these difficulties. The Turks staying in the camp to collect the spoil, they entered the Queen's houses, where they found more than forty wounded, who [65] could not stir, and began to kill them (*fazer a gazua nelles*). A Portuguese, when he saw this, determined not to allow them to enjoy that satisfaction, but to die and revenge himself on them. He raised himself and crept on all fours, with a lighted match that lay handy, and went to where the powder was, and fired it. The house blew up, none escaping, for D. Christovão had a very large store of powder, which he had made during the winter, and this was kept in the Queen's houses, as the most watertight. It is probable that this cavalier set fire to the house less because the Turks were killing those who were already dead, than in order to prevent them using the powder with which they might have done great hurt, for there was much of it.

[65]

Of how the Moors, following D. Christovão, found him, and seized him, and of How he Died.

D. Christovão and the fourteen Portuguese with him, marching all that night, travelled with heavy labour, for they were all wounded and very weary. They had therefore [66] to leave the road they followed, and enter a shady valley, with a very thick growth of trees, to take some rest. As the morning was near, and there was great fear of discovery by the enemy who were in pursuit, having, as I say, left the path, they entered the bottom of the valley in the most solitary possible place, where they found a little water that flowed from a water-fall. They got D. Christovão off his mule to dress his wounds, which up to now they had not had time to do; his companions, not having wherewith to do it, killed the mule D. Christovão rode, and taking the fat, dressed with it his wounds, and also the wounds of those among them that needed it. When the Moors captured the camp some would not halt, but followed us relentlessly; on the road by which D. Christovão escaped there went twelve Turks on foot and twenty Arabs on horse-back, eager to capture him; at dawn they were beyond where he lay, and not finding him, they returned. Reaching the point where D. Christovao turned into the thicket, an old woman came out of the wood, looking as if she could hardly stand, and ran across the road; the Moors, to learn her news, tried to catch her, and followed her into the wood, without capturing her, as she ran from one thicket to another. When she got to the valley she crossed it, running fast, and entered among the trees where D. Christovão and the Portuguese lay. As the Moors followed with pertinacity, they would not abandon the pursuit, and thus came on D. Christovão, and taking him by surprise, with loud cries of "Mafamede," captured him. One of these [D. Christovão's companions] who was but slightly wounded, hid in the thicket and escaped, and from him we heard the story of the capture. It is impossible that that [67] old woman can have been any one save the devil, as she vanished from among them and was never seen again. This astonished the Moors greatly, who, from what they told us afterwards, considered that "Mafamede" had sent her to direct them; they returned contented with their prize, as they at once recognised D. Christovão by the arms he bore; thus they went with him, making him many mocks by the way, and giving him but evil treatment. Thus they brought them before the King, who was very pleased with the victory, with more than one hundred and sixty Portuguese heads before his tent: for he had offered a reward to any Moor who would cut off the head of a Portuguese, and his men, to gain it, brought him those they found on the field. When D. Christovão reached his tent, that dog ordered the heads of the Portuguese to be shown him, to grieve him; telling him whose they were, and that here were those with whom he had designed to conquer his country, and that his madness was clear in his design; and that for this boldness he would do him a great honour. This was to order him to be stripped, with his hands tied behind him, and then cruelly scourged, and his face buffeted with his negroes' shoes; of his beard he made wicks, and covering them with wax lighted them; with the tweezers that he had sent him, he ordered his eyebrows and eyelashes to be pulled out: saying that he had always kept them for him, as he and his followers did not use them. After this, he sent him to all his tents and his Captains for his refreshment, where many insults were heaped on him, all of which he bore with much patience: giving many thanks to God for bringing him to this, after allowing him to reconquer [68] one hundred leagues of Christian country. After they had diverted themselves with him they returned to the King's tent, who with his own hand cut off his head, it not satisfying him to order it to be cut off. After it had been cut off, in that very place where his blood was spilt, there started a spring of water which gave health to the sick, who bathed in it, which they understood the wrong way. That very day and moment, in a monastery of friars, a very large tree which stood in the cloisters was uprooted, and remained with its roots in the air and its branches underneath, the day being very calm and still; and as it appeared to them that this event was not without mystery, they noted the day and the hour, and that they were all present to give witness. Afterwards, when they heard of the defeat and death of D. Christovão, they found that the tree was uprooted on the very day and hour that he was killed. After it had died, the friars cut up part for use in the monastery; six months later, the very day we gave battle to the King of Zeila and defeated him — in which battle he was slain and the kingdom freed — that very day the tree raised itself, planted its roots in the earth whence they had been drawn, and at the same moment threw out green leaves. The friars, seeing this great mystery, with great wonder, noted the day and hour it happened, knowing nothing of what was passing in the kingdom. When they heard of what had taken place, they found that it was the very day, as I say, that was the signal of freedom for so many Christian people. When they told us this, as the monastery lay on the road to Massowa, whither after the [69] freeing of the country we were travelling, we all went to the monastery to see the tree and to bear witness. I saw it, with many of its roots exposed, all cut as the friars said, and it had only recently become green. As it was a great tree, it was wonderful that it could stand on the ground with so few roots below the earth. When, after the King of Zeila had cut off D. Christovão's head, that fact became known in the tents of the Turks, they were very enraged, and went angrily to the King, and asked him why he had thus killed the Portuguese Captain without telling them: because, as the Grand Turk had heard of his bravery, they could have taken him nothing from that country which would have pleased him more, that they would have taken him as a proof of their great victory to receive a reward from the Turk. They were so offended that they quitted him, taking the Portuguese to carry with them. The next day, when they started, there was one Portuguese, who had escaped, the less; he afterwards joined us, so that they went back with twelve and D. Christovão's head. They embarked for Azebide, where was the Governor of all the Straits, with three thousand Turks, of which body they formed a part. Two hundred were left with the King of Zeila, because they filled up the vacancies of those who were killed in the battle from among the others, as this number was granted by the Grand Turk in exchange for his tribute. The King stayed three days at that place, with great content at the victory, for such is their custom, making great festival; and as it appeared to him that we were entirely destroyed, and that those who remained of us would be lost in that country, among those mountains, [70] where we could not find our way, he determined to visit his wife and sons, whom he had not seen for a long time, who were in his city on the shores of the lake whence the Nile flows, the most rich and fertile country that ever was seen. This he did, leaving in that country his Captains, with troops to retake possession of the land he had lost; for of us he took no count, bad or good, but the Lord God chose to show His great pity.

[70]

Of how some one hundred and twenty Portuguese collected with the Queen, and of how the Preste arrived at the Hill of the Jews, where the Queen, his Mother, and the Portuguese were awaiting him.

It happened, in our flight, that the Queen was escaping in front with her women, very sorrowful, as it may be supposed she would be; the Portuguese were in her rear, wounded and scattered, and behind all were ten or twelve who could hardly travel. Helping them, there went two Portuguese who were less wounded than they, urging them on and remaining in their company. One was called Fernão Cardoso, the other Lopo de Almansa. At nine or ten hours of the next day, they saw following them many Moors on foot and two horsemen. When the pursuers drew near, they determined to die, and try and save their comrades, who were in front of them, wounded. These they told to travel as fast as they could, for they would defend them or perish. So they both turned back against the Moors, and they carried bucklers and pikes. When they came near the two Moorish horsemen, who were the nearest, they tried to attack them; but the Moors drew [71] back, awaiting the footmen to capture them, telling them to give up their arms and surrender, and they would not kill them. When they saw so many opponents, they thought that the Moors could destroy them with arrows and stones only, without coming to push of pike or sword; and, since they could not approach them to do what they wanted, that therefore they should yield. Maybe they [the opponents] would turn back with them [as captives], as the others were not in sight. That, even if the Moors tortured them, they would never confess that the other Portuguese had gone on; that in this way they might save their comrades by dying themselves, for they could not escape that. With this determination, they went up to the horsemen; Lopo de Almanza, who knew somewhat of the language, calling out that they would surrender, and that they should receive their arms. Advancing to surrender, it would seem that Our Lady inspired them, for they called out one to the other and simultaneously, "Holy Mary! they will slay us with our own weapons." With these words, they attacked the horsemen, who were now near, and knocked down both at the first strokes; one dead, the other wounded in the arm. When they fell, their horses stood still without moving, and the footmen, numerous as they were, began to fly: which seems a great and evident miracle. Then the two cavaliers mounted the horses of the Moors, and, after making a feint of following the footmen a short way, went in search of their comrades; and, mounting the worst wounded double, told them what had happened. They were much astonished at this success, and very joyful to see them: for they thought they were already dead or captives. Thus all escaped, these two running the risk of death to save the others. Our Lady, seeing their intention, inspired them at such a time with this courage. In this way they saved their comrades, and also those in front; for if these Moors had followed them they would have slain [72] all, for they had neither arms nor breath. Thus they journeyed with abundant labour until reaching the Queen; and it was very evident in what great tribulation they fled. We did not halt until we reached a very rough hill, and as we could travel no further we rested there. The greater number of the Portuguese who escaped collected here, and the following day came the thirty Portuguese with the horses, who had not heard of our disaster. When they had joined us, and saw our condition, and heard of the loss of D. Christovão, our lamentation was so great as to cause pity, and we could not be comforted. What we all felt most was, not to have news of D. Christovão, beyond how badly he was wounded. The Queen sent several scouts along the roads, and to the thickets, to gather, if possible, any news, and to guide any Portuguese found concealed. We were here for several days, waiting for news to reach us. We assembled round the Queen, to the number of one hundred and twenty men, among whom was the man who escaped when D. Christovão was captured, who told us of what I have already related; and also the one who escaped from the camp of the Moors, who informed us of the martyrdom of D. Christovão, and his death, as already told. Our feelings on hearing this can be believed. There returned a scout of the Queen's, who told us that Manuel da Cunha, with fifty Portuguese, had taken another road, not knowing whither they were going. They reached the country of the Barnaguais, where they were welcomed, and where they remained till they heard news of us and the Queen; she with her women felt the greatest grief at the fate of D. Christovão, whom they lamented as if he had been her son. The following day she sent for us all, and made us a speech, consoling us for our great loss, [73] and for our contrary fortune; and this in very discreet and virtuous words. We asked the patriarch to reply for us all, encouraging her; and she was pleased, saying that the courage of the Portuguese was very great. It was determined at our council to go to the hill of the Jews, and there await the Preste, who had already been informed that the hill was his. We started the next day, and were very well received by the Captain of the hill, and provided with all necessaries. Ten days later, the Preste arrived, bringing very few people; so few that, had not D. Christovão captured the hill, it would have been impossible for us to have joined him, or for the kingdom to have been restored.

Of the Reception the Portuguese gave the Preste; and of how after the Meetings we deter mined to all go and revenge the Death of D. Christovão.

When we heard that the Preste was at the foot of the hill we went to receive him, a Mass Priest who was with us bearing in his hands the banner of Compassion. When we reached him, seeing us like this, and so few in number, and hearing of the death of D. Christovão and of our defeat, he showed such affliction as was to be anticipated, for he came full of desire to see D. Christovão from the fame that had reached him; and the affliction he showed, surely for a son and heir he would not have shown more. He gave us all much honour and welcome, with princely words, telling us not to feel strangers in that country, but to look on it as our own, for the kingdom and he himself belonged to the King, our lord, and his brother. He at once provided us with all necessaries, gave us all mules to ride – for, after the late defeat, we had come here on foot — he gave to all, too, silken tunics and breeches, for such is the country wear, to every two men a tent, and servants in abundance to attend us, carpets and mattresses, and all we needed. We were here all December, both because the Preste wished to celebrate Christmas here, and also to collect the men who daily flocked to him: there assembled here eight thousand foot and five hundred horse. When we saw this force we went to the Preste, and begged him to help us to avenge the death of D. Christovão. The Preste, although he desired this, still was very fearful, as we were so few; but he determined to attempt it, and sent to summon the Portuguese who had fled to the territory of the Barnaguais, and to fetch the arms D. Christovão had left on the hill where we found the Queen, where as the [75] place was secure, he left our surplus weapons, which were a great help to us, as we had now but very few. During this time we made a good deal of powder, as the man whom D. Christovão had with him for this, escaped with us, by the favour of our Lord, to make it in the time of such need: for on this hill of the Jews there is much saltpetre and sulphur, and all that is necessary. During the whole of January the Preste was here, getting ready and awaiting the Portuguese. The latter were not then in the country of the Barnaguais; for it appeared to them that we were all dead, and that they could not join the Preste; they therefore journeyed to Massowa, to embark for India, should any of our foists come there. When this information regarding them arrived, and the weapons which were on the hill came, the Preste determined to go and seek the Moors; for he learned that the Turks who had come to his assistance had returned, and that he had only the two hundred, who were always with him, and his own followers.

Of how the Preste began to march with the Portuguese and found the King of Zeila encamped on the Lake of the Nile; and of the method the King of Zeila adopted to kill the Captain of the Preste's Camp.

Forming our ranks, we began our march on Shrove Tues-day, February 6th, 1543, with eight thousand footmen with bows and bucklers, and five hundred horse, all very fine and well-found men, and one hundred and twenty Portuguese, — some maimed, with wounds still open, who refused [76] to stay behind, as they were bent on vengeance or on death in the attempt. We bore before us the banner of Holy Compassion; the Preste had sought to appoint one of us Captain, but we desired none save the banner or himself to lead us, for it was not to be anticipated that we should follow another, having lost what we had lost. Thus we marched, leaving the Queen, his mother, on that hill, to have no incumbrance. On our way we heard that a Captain of the King of Zeila was on the road by which we must travel, in a lordship called Ogara, who had three hundred horse and two thousand foot; the Captain of them was called Miraizmao. We reached the place one morning early, and the Preste fell on with fifty horse in the van. By this attack the Moors were defeated, the Captain and many of them slain, and many [77] prisoners captured; from them we learned that the King of Zeila was with his wife and sons on the bank of the lake whence the Nile springs, about five days' march, at our speed, from where we were. We continued marching until we caught sight of it; — it is so large that we could see it from a dis-

47

tance of six or seven leagues. When we came in sight of the Moors we pitched our camp opposite theirs. They were amazed to learn that the Preste and the Portuguese had came in search of them after the great defeat; this put them in some fear. They began at once to prepare as best they could; they understood well that we had only come to avenge the past. And because we had news of the Portuguese who had been to Massowa, but had not found shipping, that hearing of us and the Preste, they were marching after us, with all speed, the Preste decided in council of all not to join battle until their arrival, as they were near us; and in that country fifty Portuguese are a greater reinforcement than one thousand natives. In the days we were awaiting them we had daily skirmishes on the plain between the armies. There were [78] now sixty mounted Portuguese, as the Preste gave them all the horses he had; they had very good fortune in the skirmishes, for there continually came out a certain Moorish Captain, who was greatly famed among them, and in whom they trusted, with two hundred horse; he was so unfortunate, that in one of his skirmishes with the Portuguese, he and twelve of his companions were killed, which was a great loss to them. The Abyssinian horse also made many sallies, seeking to impress us; the Captain-General of the camp, by name Azemache Cafilao, did marvels with his horse on these days, for nothing could show outside the King of Zeila's camp without being raided by this Captain; in this the Moors always had the worst, losing both their flocks and their lives. When the Moor saw how brave our Captain was, he determined to make a great effort to kill him by treachery. He sent for one of his cavaliers, and told him to send the Captain a message bearing the air of a challenge: a message to summon him to one side of the camp where was a small stream, he remaining on one bank and the Abyssinian on the other; in some thickets on his bank four or five Turks were to conceal themselves by night with matchlocks, that, while the message was being delivered, they might fire their matchlocks at him and kill him. And thus it was: at early dawn the Turks hid in the thickets, and at daybreak two horsemen, with a white flag, rode to the edge of the small stream, and called for the Captain of the camp by name. Our men ran up to know what it was, but the Moors would not say aught, save to call the Captain of the camp, as they had something of importance to tell him. When the Captain, who was already mounted, heard this, he came towards the stream with a large following, but when he saw there were [79] but two Moors, he ordered his men to halt, thinking the men wanted to come over to us, or else give some useful information, and that to deceive their own side they had come through the thickets; he went forward with but two horsemen in whom he trusted. When he came within speech of them, he asked what they wanted, and while the Moors were feigning some tale, the Turks all fired their matchlocks at him; when they saw him fall over his saddlebow, they turned and went off at full gallop. The Turks had saddled horses hard by, and on them they escaped. When our horsemen saw that the Moors were galloping off, they came up fearing treachery; and, when they saw the Captain dead in the arms of his two companions, they started to pursue the Moors, who were going off untouched; but so many came out to assist them, that our men had to return with the dead Captain. At this they made great lamentation, the Preste above all, both as he had married one of his cousins, and because he was a very brave man. With him the Abyssinians began to lose their courage, so much so that many advised retreat, victory seeming impossible. When the Preste heard of this, and found it true, he sent for them, and determined, as the Portuguese delayed so long, to give battle the next day, as he felt that if he waited longer, all his men would disperse through fear.

Of how the Preste and the King of Zeila fought a Battle in which the Moors were defeated and the King slain.

By early morning we were all in our ranks, and we said a prayer before the banner of the Holy Compassion (Sancta Misericordia), begging our Lord to have it [compassion] on [80] us, and give us vengeance on, and victory over, our enemies. After a general confession by a Mass priest, who absolved us, we arose and advanced against the enemy, we leading the van and that banner, or we following it [? e esta bandeyra ou nós com ella]. With us were two hundred and fifty Abyssinian horse and three thousand five hundred foot; in the rear came the Preste with another two hundred and fifty horse, and with all the rest of the foot. In this order we attacked the enemy, who also advanced in two battles, the King of Zeila in person in the van, with two hundred Turks, matchlockmen, six hundred horse and seven thousand foot. Those in the van attacked on both flanks; in the rear came his Captain, called Guança Grade, with six hundred horse and seven thousand foot, who like the van attacked heavily. The Portuguese, seeing that the Turks were defeating us, charged them, slaying many and driving the rest back; for the Portuguese horse, who were sixty, worked marvels, and the Abyssinians, ashamed to see them fight thus, threw themselves in so vigorously that they left a track as they went. When the King saw that his men were losing ground, he in person led them on, encouraging them, and with him was his son, a young man, helping him; they came so near that he was recognised by the Portuguese, who, seeing him close, fired at him with their matchlocks. As all things are ordered by the Lord God, He permitted that one ball should strike him in the breast, and he fell over his saddlebow and left the press; when his followers knew that he was wounded to the death, they lost heart and took to flight. When the Captain of [81] the Turks saw that the Moors were giving way, he determined to die; with bared arms, and a long broadsword in his hand, he swept a great space in front of him; he fought like a valiant cavalier, for five Abyssinian horsemen were on him, who could neither make him yield nor slay him. One of them attacked him with a javelin; he wrenched it from his hand, he houghed another's horse, and none dared approach him. There came up a Portuguese horseman, by name Gonçalo Fernandes, who charged him spear in rest and wounded him sorely; the Turk grasped it [the spear] so firmly, that before he could disengage himself the Moor gave him a great cut above the knee that severed all the sinews and crippled him; finding himself wounded, he drew his sword and killed him. All this while our men were pursuing the Moors, chiefly the Portuguese, as they could not glut their revenge; they mainly followed the Turks, as against them they were most enraged; of the two hundred not more than forty escaped, who returned to the King's wife. When she heard that her husband was dead, she fled with the three hundred horse of her guard and these forty Turks, taking with her all the treasure that her husband had captured from the Preste, which was not small. She escaped, as our people followed those on the battle-field and in the camp so relentlessly that they thought of nothing else; and they gave quarter to none, save women and children, whom they made captives. Among these were many Christian women, which caused the greatest possible pleasure and contentment: for some found sisters, others daughters, others their wives, and it was for them no small delight to see them delivered from such captivity. So great was their pleasure, that they came to kiss our feet and worship us; they gave us the credit of the battle, saying that through us they saw [82] that day. When the spoil, which was not small, had been collected, the Preste pitched his camp on the shore of the lake, for the country abounds in supplies. After the booty had been secured, there came to the Preste one of his Captains, by name Azemache Calite, a youth, with the head of the King of Zeila in his teeth, and he at full stretch of his horse with great pleasure; for this youth and the Barnaguais, who knew him [the King of Zeila] best, followed him, and this youth got up to him first and finished killing him, and cut off his head; he took his head so eagerly to the Preste on account of the promises he had made, which were great: if any Abyssinian brought the head, to marry him to his sister; if a Portuguese, to show him great favour. When the Preste received the Moor's head he enquired into the truth, and found that the Portuguese had mortally wounded him, and that this Captain did not merit his sister for bringing the head, as he did not kill him; thus he did not give his sister to that man, nor did he reward the Portuguese, as it was not known who wounded him; had he known, he would have fulfilled his promise. He ordered that the head of the late King of Zeila should be set on a spear, and carried round and shown in all his country, in order that the people might know that he was indeed dead who had wrought them such evils. It was first taken to the Queen, to be sent thence to the other places; and thus she was avenged by her pleasure for the sadness past. At this time the Portuguese who had been to Massowa arrived at the place where the Queen was; she determined in her satisfaction to join her son, and the Portuguese accompanied her; they were well received by the Preste, who supplied them with all necessaries, and made great festivities for the Queen. We remained in great pleasure, seeing each day the Abyssinians delighting in that victory, and in the liberty in which they found themselves. There died four Portu- [83] guese in the battle: João Correa, Francisco Vieyra, Francisco Fialho, and a Gallician.

Table des matières